MR. BLUE SKY AND THE WHITE DOVE

AN ANTHOLOGY OF POEMS

DR. GOKEN GEYI

I dedicate this book to all those who love to spread the
beauty of poetry. And to those who love to spread Love
and Peace through poetry.

Contents

Contents

Contents

Contents

Preface

Since I remember myself I always love to read and write. As a young girl i use to write whatever comes to my mind. I don't remember what, why and how a young girl was writing but still I can feel the "Feel" while writing. Still writing is the only thing that brings me soul satisfaction. I feel empty, disconnected, and vulnerable when I am not writing. So, being a grown up woman also I don't know what, why and how I am writing but while I am writing poetry the "Feel" is so pure and divine. When i read poetries i feel a deep connection with the lines, words, emotions and sentiments in the poem. As if someone has understood my sentiments and emotions without being with me physically. Through poetry I can feel a spiritual connection with everything and with some souls who share similar abstract intellectualism with me. The beauty of poetry touches my soul and makes my tired mind relaxed and light. Then I realise that like me there must me many soul who love to feel the beauty of poetry. And there must be some souls who need to feel the 'connection' and who wants to feel the "connection". For me "Poetry" is the most beautiful way to spread the "Feel" and the "Connection" among the human beings.

So the eagerness to share the beauty and power of poetry motivates me to write poems. My mother Late Mrs Gotam kato Geyi, my grandmother Late Mrs Debi Geyi Kato and my elder sister Late Mrs Gorik Geyi Chetri always encourage me to write. These Ladies were the only people who have understood that the only thing i love to do with my soul is writing. They all are gone now. When I write poems I feel the pain of losing them is becoming less and i feel that they are also joyfully cheering my poems. I feel they are around me, near me, encouraging me to face the pain boldly. And I feel that I am sharing the beauty of my poems with them also. This feeling motivate me more to write poems. Therefore, I love to write till my last breath. What I will be writing, how I will be writing and where I will be writing i do not know but I will write. Even if only one reader would feel the connection and the feel that itself will be a huge success for this poor poet.

Dr. Goken Geyi

I know a place..!

Far away from disagreements and disputes

I know a place...!

Where my soul sings to yours..!

Far away from intellectual Discourses and conflicts

I know a place..!

Where my heart talks to yours...!!

Far away from words and reasons

I know a place...!

Where my mind feels yours..!!

Far away from cacophonies and white noises

I know a place...!

Where my silence meets yours...!!!!!

The Royal Garments..!!

She became a Hadassah...her time to meet the king arrived..!

It's time for her to meet the king of the kings..!

It's time for her to put the 'Royal Garments'...

As her time arrived to stand in front of the king..!!

It's time for her to put on the 'royal garments'...

The royal garments jewelled with king's royal blood..

The royal garments jewelled with the king's words...

The king's living words...!

It's time for her to put on the royal garments to win the king...!!

I'm someone's waiting..!!

Someone is waiting me...I'm someone's Waiting..!

Someone Loves me...I'm someone's Love..!!

Mr. Blue Sky...my Blue Bridge...,

Will you take me to him..??!!

To him who is waiting me...waiting me beyond...

Beyond the sky..!!!

You'll come to take me..!

And one day you tell me you love me....

Then, I know why I never know Love..!

And one day you tell me pain will be over....

Then, I realize I was living a 'Pain'...!!!

And one day you tell me...

You'll come to take me...!

Then I realise I'm still not born..!!!

When you hold my hand..!!

When you hold my hand....

As if difficulties will slip away..!

As if flowers will bloom on my way..!

When you hold my hand...

As if stars will shine in the day..!!!

Our Love songs...!

One day you and I will make the stars dance...

Dance on our Love songs..!!

One day you and I will make the sun melt...!

Make the sun melt with our Love Songs..!

One day you and I will make the Heaven Smile...

Make the Heaven smile with our Love Songs..!!!

You're the Reality..!

They bring me noise...And take away my peace..!

You bring me songs...Then you become my song..!

They bring me distractions...And takes away my quietude..!

You bring me purposes...Then you become my purpose..!

They bring me shadows....And play with my hope..!!

You bring me the 'Reality'...Then you become my 'Reality'...!!!!

Living the Unlived..!

Now my words don't go unheard..!

Now my tears don't go unnoticed..!

Since you come to my life....,

My words are heard....my tears are seen..!

Unsaid is being understood..!

Now I'm living the unlived..!!

You're my waiting..!!

Your smile put gladness in my heart..!

Your Blue gentleness is my waiting..!

But your absence troubled my soul...

As if I'm engulfed by sadness..!!

Though sadden, I wait for you..!

I'm waiting you to sprinkle drops of love on me..!

My voice is drying by weeping in fear of losing you..!

You're my waiting...!

Mr. Blue Sky...! I'm waiting for you..!!

My Blue Bridge

In your blueness I see the true light..!

You're the living light of my Life..!

In your blue humble vastness I see

My resting place..!

You're the refuge of my soul..!!

Mr. Blue Sky...you're my Blue Bridge..!

In you I see a way...., a way leading me to my

Loved ones whom I lose...!!!

The White Hibiscus..!

She is unnurtured...she is obstructed...

But she grows and Bloom..!

I saw her this morning...

She was as if smiling..!

Her white purity stands high...

The white hibiscus shines...!

She is in my gate....Blooming...!!!

She is as if proclaiming her winning..!!!

A Butterfly in my garden..!!

You're visiting me again..!

I thought you've gone far away..!

I thought you've forgotten the way...

And Me..!!

Have you brought me a message...???

Or a story..??!!

Tell me my friend...I'm here...

And I'm listening...!!!

Beautiful Saviour..!

When they intent to harm...You take me out of the storm..!

When they betray...You hold me from going astray..!

When they make my life a hade...You take me into your
shade..!

When they shattered my Hope...You shower your Love..!

When they humiliate me...You take my shame..!!!

Handsome stalker...!

Yesterday I was praising the stars...

Tonight suddenly you spread your handsome calm Light..!

You become so bright...so clear...And big..!

But you seem jealous...Jealous of the stars..!

You drive them away...Away from your shine..!

O, Moon..! You're such a stalker..!

You're a stalker...But a handsome stalker..!

Wherever I go...you follow me..!!!!!!

With You..!

When Morning comes...

I dream to spend my day with you..!

When night comes...

I dream to spend my night with you..!

When poetry comes to my mind...

I dream to recite it with you..!

When the Moon and the stars smile at night...

I dream to smile them back with you..!!!

Again..!!

Since I'm feeling you in my feel...

I can smell again..!

Since I'm thinking you in my thoughts...

I can see Love again..!

Since I'm getting your aura...

I can feel the melody again..!!!!

I will be back...He said..!!

Here pain is so unbearable...I'm tired...

Please take me with you....

"Life is meant to be so...you're in the fallen World.."

He said...!

Take me with you now...

"Not now..! Wait.., it's not your time...

I'll be back to take you with me." He said..!!

Where..???!!

"Beyond the Blue Sky...where there is no pain"...!!

He said...!!!

I wonder if...!!

Seeing the blooming of the flowers...

I wonder if you're getting its fragrance..!!

Listening the singing of the wind...

I wonder if you're feeling the breeze..!!

Loving your memories...

I wonder if you're sympathising my Love..!

Watching a trail I wonder if it would lead you to Me..!!!!

She is back..!!!

Oh..! She is back..! Back with her darkness..!

Her darkness is so dark..!

She is back...the darkness is back...!

She is so dark...her darkness is stealing my light..!

She is back...! And she is dark..!!!

White Doves..!!!

It would be wonderful if I've doves..!

Doves..., lots of doves....white doves...,

Cloud like white doves..!!!

It would be wonderful if I can see them fly...

Flying around me like the white clouds..!

Yes..! it would be wonderful if I've lots of

White doves...!

White doves...cloud like white doves..!!!!!

Come back to me..!!

Its dark again...frightening clouds are here again..!

I'm scared...I'm lonely again..!!

Where are you Mr Blue Sky...??!!

Please come back to me..!

I'm scared of dark clouds...

Come back to me and hold my hands...

And take me in your embrace..!!

My Mr. Blue Sky come back to me..!!!!

Then...!

When days were cruel I cry...

I cry with my heart and soul..!!

'Then'....i was a tear...!!

When days were beautiful and kind...

I love with my heart and soul...!

'Then'....I was a Love...!

Soul mate...!

In the midst of noise she met the soul of the Silence...

She loved the silence with her soul...

The soul of the silence loved her back..!

So, her soul and the soul of the silence are soul mate now..!

In the midst of hatred she met the soul of Love..!

She loved the Love with her soul...

The soul of Love loved her back...!

So, her soul and soul of the Love are soul mate now...!!!!

The Key...!

As if someone has hidden my happiness in a box....

As if someone has hidden the key to open that box...!

As if you've brought me back the key...

As if I've opened the box...!!

Can we be friends...??

Like me are you also searching for a friend..??

Even if you don't say anything I've seen your eyes..!

If you still haven't met the one you're searching...

Dear cloud...oh! my dear cloud...

Then, can we be friends...??!!

I'm scare..!

I'm scare....like you these birds will also leave me..!

I'm scare....like you these butterflies will also betray me..!

I'm scare...like you these flowers will also humiliate me...!

I'm scare ....you'll make my friends like you..!!!!!

I wouldn't waste my tears...!

I let people hurt me...I let people betray me...!

I let people show their evils...

So that when they become

a 'gone dear' one day...I wouldn't waste my tears...!!!

Bring me back my Love..!

Before I lost my mind...

Bring me back the memories I treasured..!

Before I lost my voice...

Bring me back the songs I sung...!

Before I lost my sight...

Bring me back the love I loved...!!!

Then I Love again...!

And then Love arrives...bringing me fantasies...!

Then, I fall in Love again...leaving my agonies...!!!

And then poetry arrives...bringing me words..!

Then, I began to write again...leaving my melancholia..!!!

Sometimes...!!

Sometimes I think....sometimes I contemplate...!

Sometimes I imagine...And sometimes I analyse..!

Sometimes i feel...sometimes I emphasize..!

Sometimes I say 'Yes'...Sometimes I say 'No'..!

Oh..! How deceptive I'm..??

How deceptive mind is....???

Sometimes I wonder what an unending fight...

A fight within....a fight with myself..!!!

You look sad tonight...!!

Tonight you're behind the clouds...you neither smile nor shine...!

Oh! My handsome stalker...you even didn't follow me..!!

You look sad tonight...very sad..!

As if the dark clouds has win...as if they've stopped you from

Smile and Shine...!!!

My handsome stalker...My Moon..! I still love you..!

I'll wait for you till you defeat the clouds..!!

You look sad tonight...But you'll smile and shine again..!!

I have spot a place

I have spot a place for you and I...

A place where sky is Blue and clear

Everywhere every time...!!

I've spot a place for you and I...

Where all 'whys'...all 'Maybes'

And all separations end...!!

Where love is in the air....

Everywhere and every time...!

I've spot a place for you and I...

Where all flowers bloom...

Everywhere and every time..!

In the loudness and shouting...!

*How many beautiful thoughts might have gone
uninterpreted...!*

In the Loudness and shouting..!!

How many love desires might have gone unlived...!

How many stories might have gone untold..!

How many abilities might have gone unproved...!

In the loudness and shouting...!!

How many tears might have gone unseen..!

How many melodies might have gone unsung..!

I dream for a place where I could resurrect them...!

A place where there will be no loudness and shouting..!!!

Next Time....!!!

Next time when you meet me...

Please come closer to me...!

Next time when you come closer to me...

Please look at me in my eyes...!

Next time when we meet again....

Please stay longer with me..!

And Please Love!

Give me your voice next time we meet...!!!

You're so intoxicating...!!

You're so intoxicating...even a sip of you makes me intoxicated..!!

You're you illusive...even a glimpse of you makes me illusive..!!

You bring me to an illusion that things were better back then...

You spread the traps of 'could haves'...!

You're debilitative too...!

Even a drop of your remembrance bring me back to the lane

Where i got stuck in the memories of pain, heartbreak

And disappointments..!

You're so deceitful...!

You bring me back pleasant memories...then suddenly you

Entrapped me to the memory lane.....

Where I don't want to walk again...!

So betraying you're....leaving me stuck there...!!

You're so clinging...!

You cling to me so tightly...keeping me away from

Even trying to be happy again..!!

Dear past....you're so intoxicating...!!!!

I'm here...!

Whenever I see you all flying together...

Whenever I listens you all singing together...

I wish I also have wings like you..!

Then I would fly with you all...

Then I would sing with you all..!

Then i would wait for you all...

And chirps like you to tell you that I'm here..!!

You are my obsession..!

Am I making you my obsession..?

Or have you already become..??!!

I don't know...but you've consume my space..

Making me unable to feel my own existence..!

You've consumed my thoughts...

Making me unable to think anything else..!

Now I understand that you become my obsession...

Yes! Mr. Blue sky you're my obsession..!!

Will you search me..??

One day when my existence cease...

Will you search me in the blooming of flowers..?

One day when I'm gone...

Will you search me in the chirping of the birds..?

One day when I'm no more...

Will you search me in the crowd..?

One day when I'm gone forever....

Will you search me in your memories...?

Tell me Mr. Handsome stalker

Then tell me Mr. handsome stalker

When will you stop your stalking..??!!

Tonight, you were behind the mountain...

But still you were watching me..!

Tell me Mr. Handsome stalker is it your way to show me

that no mountain can stop you from being the

'Handsome stalker' of mine..??!!

Or are you befriending with the mountains to

Know my whereabouts..??!!

O Moon! When you'll stop your stalking..??!!

Are you the golden bridge..??

I've a lover..! He is waiting me 'There'..!!

There..! That side..! And I'm 'Here'...

Here...! This side..!! Waiting for him..!!

Oh! Colourful Rainbow will you take me to him..?

And tell me... "Are you the Golden Bridge"...??

Connecting 'This Side' to 'That Side'...!!!!

She is gone..!!

She is gone...she is no more in 'Here'..!

She is gone to a place called 'There'....

A place no one knows where..!

Where this place 'There' is no one knows..!

But she is gone..!

When she was 'Here' we never realise her presence..!

But she is gone now....never to be back again..!

Gone with her presence...leaving her absence with us..!

She is gone...!!!!!!

Lullaby..!!

I will find the most beautiful flower for you my baby..!

And I asked the garden for the most beautiful flower....

Garden replied; "woman..! You've the most beautiful flower..."!

So I don't bring back any flower...And how can I...??

Flowers themselves say you're the most beautiful flower..!!

Then I'll find the most beautiful bead for you my baby..!

And I asked the beads for the most beautiful bead...

Beads replied; "woman..! You've the most beautiful bead..."!

So I don't bring back any bead...And how can I..??!!

Beads themselves say that you're the most beautiful bead...!!!!

I smile...she smiles back..!!

One day I met her...I smile she smiles back..!

But my smile failed to deceive her..!

"Life still hurts"...? Is past still hurting you...? She asked..!

Yes...it still hurts..!

Tell me what am I suppose to do with all the hurts..???

I Replied...! She smiles back...

And said "Don't waste your hurt...create more poetry with it..!

"Hurt hurts unbearably..."! I said..!

Poetry replied; "My love..! But hurt plants seeds of poetry in you..."!

Sometimes I wish..!

Sometimes I wish I was without senses...

My senses bring me pain...!

Sometimes I wish I was without desires...

My desires bring me disdain...!

Sometimes I wish I was without dreams...

My dreams bring me illusive hope..!

Sometimes I wish I never had this life...

My Life brings me breath without hope..!!!

A becoming..!

Since I fall in love with you...

I'm walking in a path that knows no destination..!

And then I become a traveller on a path without destination..!

Since I fall in love with you...

I began to love the 'way' more than the destination..!

Since i fall in love with you...

I'm dreaming a dream that knows no ending..!

I'm meeting you in my dreams..!

I began to Love the dreams more than you..!

And then I become a dreamer of a dream

that knows no ending..!

The ways are without you...days are without you..!

But since I fall in love with you...

My love..! I'm waiting a 'wait' that do not know any 'bounding'..!!

· 47 ·

As if nothing will change...!

It was as if everything was slow and

as if everything will never grow..!

It was as if nothing will change..!

But suddenly everything change and grow..!

Then one day I realised everything has grown

And changed..!

Everything was gone...I realised..!

Nothing was same...I realised...!

But it was still as if nothing will change..!

Then I pray...!

When I think about a stream I wonder...

"Is she searching for the river..."?!

Then I pray that she meet the river..!!

When I think about a river I wonder.....

"Is she searching for the sea..."???

Then I pray that she meet the sea..!!

When I think about the sea I wonder...

"Is she searching for the Ocean"...??

Then I pray that she meet the Ocean..!!!

Because I love to love...!

One day I met life she asked me...

You're still alive..?...How..?

"Because i love to love..."

"Because I believe in creation not in dying..."!!

Said I....!!

"Don't you feel lonely"..? Life questioned..!

'Never'...I said...! How..? She said..!

'Because I've my words...it keeps me alive

So that I could create..!!!

A Short visit..!

I was young and without pain..!

I was running and laughing..!

There was no tiredness..!!

I was so light...as if I was a feather...!

I was running as if a feather was floating in the air..!

I was so happy as if I became the happiness myself..!

No haunting memories inside my head...

And no heartache..!!!!

My head was without memory..!

My heart was without pain..!

I was so new...I was a new creature...!

I was a born again Heart and Mind..!

I was a new heart...a new mind and a new spirit...!

Everything was new 'There'...my heart, my mind...

MR. BLUE SKY AND THE WHITE DOVE

My memories...my senses...!!

It was as if everything became one...!!!!!!

An Encounter...!!

I met her one day...And asked...

Are you long...or are you short...??!!

I'm neither long nor short.....I'm unpredictable...!!

She said...!

Tell me; "are you beautiful...? or You're ugly..??

I'm neither beautiful nor ugly...I'm what you make me..!!

Then, 'Are you colourful..? Or colourless...?

I'm neither colourless nor colourful...

My dear..! Choose your colours wisely...

Because I'm a reflection....your reflection...." she said..!

Are you a healer...? Or a teacher...??? I said..!!

I'm neither a healer nor a teacher...!

I'm only a memory your choices create..."!!! Life replied...!!!!

Moon was my sun..!!

Moon has brightened the nights...

As if he was trying to defeat the sun..!

So bright the nights were i was perplexed..!

Nights and Days became same..!

Nights were bright as Day...!

Those were the days when the 'Moon' was my sun...!!!!

They are gone..!

We talk...we talk a lot..! We laugh...we laugh a lot...!

We count the stars at night...we feel the breeze in the evening..!

Together, we defeat the sadness...everything was so pure...!

Everything was so innocent...!

I still talk...I still laugh...!

I still watch the moon...! I still count the stars...!

And yes! I still feel the breeze...!

But nothing is pure....nothing is innocent...!!

Everything is still here but they are gone...

They're gone from everything...Purity and innocence is gone..!!!!

Till I'm here...!!!

Till I'm here let me be a tree...a tree watered by life giving water...!

A tree, bearing fruits throughout the year...!

Till I'm here let me be a fragrance...a fragrance spreading scent of

Love and peace...!

Till I'm here let me be a letter...a letter, every lovers wait to read...!

A letter, each heart wanted to preserve...!!

Till I'm here let me be a light...a light, defeating the dark and fear...!

A light, making the darkness shine..!!!!!

The third story...!!

We walked on the path of Love...

Walking the "Love Path" we build stories...

Stories sheltering Love and Innocence...!

Stories holding memories...

Your story and mine..!!!

Then, we arrived on the path of separation...

You walked away with your story...

And I, with mine...!

But...the "Third story" walked away by herself..!

She walked away from "Us"

with her untold and unheard story..!

Sheltering the "silence".....

And "Incompleteness" the third story walked away...!

Choosing her own path she has gone...

Gone unshared, unlived and unfinished...!

I Lost it...!

That deep wound...that dark part...!

That heavy sadness...that haunting memories...!

Being with you I lost it...!

I lost them all...!

These are gone...! Yes! All are gone..!

Your love drives them away...!!!

Take me with you..!!

On the edge of this realm when I'll reach..!

On the verge of last moment when I'll reach..!

At the last breathe of my Life when I'll reach..!

Come to me and take me with you...!!!

Taken or stolen...??

Her innocence taken...!

Taken or stolen..??

She herself never knows..!!

Her wings clipped...her dreams shackled..!

Standing somewhere...where...?

That too she herself never knows...!

She wonders where it went..??

Wonders who've stolen her innocence...??

Confused...she wonders...wonders that was it

Taken or stolen...????!!!

Like a Horizon..!

Watching the sky meeting the mountain...I'm elated..!

Watching the sky meeting the ocean...I'm elated..!

As if you and I are meeting....

But, then I realise it is just a horizon...!

And like a horizon our meeting is just a mirage...!

The "meetings" are unreal....

Unreal and illusive but beautiful...!!

The soft-whisper...!!

On the hill top I was standing then "He" passed by me..!

Before him a furious wind come...so furious it was..

It split the hills...and shattered the rocks...!

I was searching "Him" in the wind...but he wasn't in it...!

Then a catastrophic "Earthquake" comes...

So catastrophic it was it split the land and parted the water...!

I was searching "Him" in the shaking..!

But he wasn't in there..!!

He passed by me....but before, again a terrifying fire come..

So terrifying it was it burnt everything on its way...!

I was searching "Him" in the fire...

But he wasn't there...!

I was tired of waiting but still I was standing there...!

Though tired waiting him...!

Then, come a soft whisper of voice...just a soft whisper of voice..

So soft it was...whole love was in its softness..!

I find the "Him" in the calm softness...!

He comes in the 'soft-whisper'..!!!

Leaving behind the mundane..!

One day you and I will travel...

Leaving behind the mundane...

We both will travel...travel all over the world...!

Together you and I will travel till our shoes will worn...!

And until our feet hurt..!

Leaving behind the mundane...

And there we'll leave the old stories and old memories..!

Yes, darling...! One day we'll travel to new places...

And together we'll create new memories...

Also we'll collect new stories...

Leaving the mundane...!

My love..! One day you and I will travel to "Land of Love"...!

Seeds of sadness..!

She was feeding herself inside..!

Like a parasite she was growing within....!

She was like a seed...

And was germinating the baby plant inside her..!

She was growing...and was becoming a tree...!

Yes! The seed of sadness bear fruits...!

And was passing the seeds to the pure and vulnerable 'hearts'...!

But still she cries...!!

I thought my heart was crowded...

But I find an empty-space there..!

And then, I found someone...

Someone inhibiting the void..!

I asked; "who are you...?"!!

"I'm Loneliness"...! She replied...!

Then I decorate her with your memories..!

But still she cries...! Cries to have you back...!

She was waiting you...

Waiting you inside the empty-space...!

Oh..! the voidness was inhabiting in her

Since very long...!

Then I told her;

"Cry but let your tears water seeds of hope..."!!!!!

It is you...!

It is you who keeps me away from crowd..!

Coming to my dream you keeps me dreaming...!

It is you who keeps me away from noises..!

Giving me words you keep me writing..!

Bringing me songs you keep me singing..!

Oh! Mr. Blue Sky...it is you who brings me voices..!

Bringing me voices you keep me listening..!

I'll dream you..!

I'll never wake up if you'll be in my dreams..!

I'll be dreaming all the time if you're in my dreams..!

If you're not there when I wake up...

Then I'll never wake up..!

I love to get lost in dreams with you...

Instead to not have you when I wake up..!

I'll dream you in my dreams...

And will never wake up...if you're not there...!!

He loved me first...!

I thought I have chosen you...I thought I've loved you...!

I thought I've found you..!

I thought I've decided to love you for eternity...!

But, then I realise you've chosen me...!

You've chosen me before I choose you...!

Then I realise it is you who loved me before I was created...!

Then I realise it is you who found me first when I was nowhere..!

Then, I understand you were calmly waiting for

my wondering soul to reach you...!!!!

You saddened me last night..!

I saw you flying alone last night....

Flying alone isn't you...!!

I heard you singing a melancholic song last night...

Singing a melancholic song isn't you...!

I saw you searching someone in despair...!

Searching someone isn't you...!

You saddened me last night my bird friend...!!!!!

Will you be there..??

Will you be there..? Will you meet me...?

I'm trying to sleep! Yes I'm trying to sleep...

so that I can meet you in my dream...!

Will you be there...there in my dream...?

Come to my dream...I'm trying to sleep...

To dream and to be with you in my dream...!!

Good bye...!

They decided to set on their own journey...

And I've a different journey..!

Our paths are different..!

So, I decided to say my 'good byes' ..!

Then, I decided to carry them in my heart..!

And decided to carry them in my prayers..!!!!

What will remain here..??

What will remain here..? When I'm gone...

When my existence end what will remain here..?

I wonder....!

I'll be gone someday...my journey will end someday!

But both the story and memory will be here..!

Here, with the stories and memories in making..!

When I'm gone my story will be making more stories..!

And my memories making more memories here

When I'll be gone 'There'...!

Some making some cry...and some making some smile..!!

And my stories doing the same making some cry and some smile..!

What will remain here..? I'm just a passerby...!

Then what will remain here...when I'm gone..!

I'll be gone someday but my stories and memories will be here...

Living in harmony with 'Tears' and 'Laughter'...!!!!

The Road...!

I have seen it many times but had never walked on it..!

Where is it..?? I don't know....!!

But it is on the left side...left side when I walk from East to West..!

I don't know where it is but whenever I see it I feel the road is

Talking to me...smiling and welcoming me...!!

Beautiful trees are in both sides of the road..!

it was so out of time zone..!

Even just watching it gives me a feeling of clarity and calmness..!

It was as if the road was a person who was conveying me a message

That it will lead me to a place where I'll live all my unlived thoughts..!

Though I don't know where it is...though I had never walked on it..!

As if it is the road that will lead me to the "Highway of Holiness"...!

As if it will lead me to my home...my eternal home..!!!

She was a Liar..!!

She was a liar...now I know she was a liar..! She lied to me about

Her life, about people ....And about situations...!

She lied to me saying people are good...good to a good person..!

She lied to me saying situations change for good..!

These all were lies...!!

Now, I know she lied to me...she was a liar...!

Hiding her sadness in her laughter...every time trying to be pleasant...

She even lied to herself..!

Now, I wonder how someone can lie so perfectly and consistently..!

She herself became a lie...!

A picture of happy and pleasant woman was a lie...!

I've seen her shedding tears whole night....everyone uses her...

Despise her...she was helpless...!

Life was cruel to her...people were cruel to her...!

But she was a liar...so she continues to lie about people and life..!

She still dares to say "they are good people"...she still dares to say

"Life is good; situations will change for good..."!

She was a liar...but always advised me not to lie..!!!

Yes! My mother was a liar..!!!

A Poet's dream...!

I dream to live in a world where all beings love one-another..!

I dream of a life that values the lives...!

The 'Haves' would sympathise the 'Haves not'...!

I dream to live in a world where people do not know deception,

Corruption, rivalry.....and lying..!

Where minds are dominated by clarity...understanding and beauty..!

Where people have hearts filled with Love, Kindness....Compassion

And thankfulness..!!!

I dream to live in a world where people do not hoard...

Where people love to share...where people value life more than things....!

Where people value love more than pleasure..!!

I'll fly away to the 'Beyond'...!

The weight of this world is trying to bury my spirit..!

But she didn't know that now I've wings..!

And I will fly away to a far place before she grabs me..!

I'll fly away and hide myself in the clouds..!

She is digging grave for me but I will fly high and swift..!

Before she buries me I'll fly away to the "Beyond"...!

The weight of life is trying to bury my spirit...!

But she didn't know that the cage is broken...

Cage of fear is no more...!!!

And I've wings to fly...fly to the "beyond"...!

My seer...I forgive everyone..!

It was hurt to forget..!

But since I'm in Love with you O! My Seer..!

I forget every hurts...And everything..!

It was hurt to forgive..!

But since I'm listening to your words

O! My Seer..! I forgive everyone...And everything..!!!!

Incense...!!

Being in your Love I began to burn incense..!

Burning incenses...I spread fragrance...the fragrance of Love..!

Being in your Love I become an incense-burner..!

Burning incenses I become incense myself..!

Spreading fragrance I become fragrance myself..!

Being in your Love I become incense...

Being in your Love I become fragrance..!!!

I'm terrified to lose you..!

Wherever I may be living....with whom I may be living...

I don't worry...And I'm not terrified...!

I'm not scared to lose anyone...

I'm not afraid to lose anything..!

But I'm terrified to lose you...

Birds, Butterflies, trees, fireflies....

And quietness I'm terrified to lose you...!!!

She was everywhere..!

She was making me scared...! I was afraid of her...I hate her...!

I was running away from her...! But she runs faster than me.......!

I don't want to see her...! But she was everywhere..!

I hate to feel her...! But she was everywhere....

And every time she was there as if she has entered inside me..!

Then, I decided to confront her...!

One day, I confronted back to her...why are you stalking me..??!!

You are not real...you're not powerful...And you're nowhere..!

I shouted to her...!!!

Yes ! You're right..! But your mind is so inviting...

Therefore, I'm everywhere....!! Fear replied..!!

A House somewhere..!!

My redeemer who loved me unconditionally...

He has built me a house...! Where..???

He and I only know..!!!

He showed me the path leading to the house..!

He is my life...He is my Truth...

And yes He himself is the way..!

He accepted me....He Loved me...!

He is the "Truth"...I and He know..!

He built a house somewhere for me....!

And He will take me to 'There' himself...!

That I and He know...!!!!!

Obscurity...!!!!

No one knows my existence..! But I exist...and will grow to a tree..!

Far away from eyes of people...I'll grow and strengthen my roots...!

Without support...without influence I'm invisible....!

But I'm growing...I'm nurturing the plants inside me...!

I'm penetrating deep inside the soil...!

In the obscurity I'm becoming a tree...a tree sheltering birds....a tree giving

Shade to the tired souls...!

For greedy and mean people I'm non-existence...And yes I want to be...

Yes, I want to be Non-exist for them..!

But in obscurity I'm nurturing the plants with Patience, wisdom and calmness..!

Far away from ill-intentioned minds the plant is growing...!!!

The plant inside me is becoming a tree in the obscurity....!!!!!!!

The Living Light...!

There she was sitting somewhere alone...she was sitting with a heavy soul..!

Soul that was chained by anger...anger conceived by wrongs done to her..!

Heart and mind was locked in a dark room...a dark room like her heavy soul..!

Though none of her fault she felt as if the burden she carries will bury her...

Bury in a grave of darkness..!

Then, she met darker souls that were heavier than hers...

Chained by heavier chain of anger..!

Some were chained by guilt some by shame and some by sadness...!

There she was sitting somewhere alone...!

But this time she was listening to the stillness...

Listening to the whisper in the stillness..!

"Be a Beacon to these heavy souls" the stillness whispers to her consciousness...!

A light flow to her soul...a living light that defeats her burdens making her light

like a feather...!

A living light flow to her soul that breaks her chain....the chain of anger..!

There she was sitting alone...this time smiling within and shining outside...!

Now she decided to carry 'The Living Light'..!

to leave the burdens and anger somewhere..!

Somewhere away from her renewed soul..!

And to be buried with the Living Light...not with the dark heavy soul...!!!!!

The Carpenter...!

Since I fall in love with Him.....

I realized I never loved anyone with my soul...!

I loved with my heart...but with my soul..??? None...!!

Since I fall in love with him i can see pathways through mountains....

I can see springs in the deserts...!

His love fills my heart with poetry..! I was scared of crowd...

I was scared of vultures around me..!

He takes me out of the crowd encircled by the vultures...!

He takes me out from the crowd encircled by wolves..!

He brings me to a place where I can feel his presence with Clarity..!

He brings me far away from the vulture and wolves...!

I thought he loves me but i never knew he knows me more than i know myself..!

I fall in love with him because he is kind and humble....!

But never knows he is the only Carpenter who can make

the key that can open all the cages and dungeons..!

As if we all become One..!!

That evening while I was walking there was no light...

Darkness had engulfed whole college campus...!

I was scared for a while...so I stopped walking..!

Standing there first I feel the darkness... Then I saw a few fireflies...!

Just in a blink few become many...and many become so many..!

They were lighting their tiny lamps...

Many of them shining and dancing together..!!!

As if they were waiting for me to shine and dance..!

Their dancing and shining ward off my fear..!

Amazed..! I smiles back..! And raise my head appreciating the creator..!

The creator...theirs and mine..!

Then, I saw thousands of stars shining above..!

Like the fireflies the stars also shine and dance together..!

As if they were also waiting for me to shine and dance..!

It was as if the fireflies become the stars..!

And the stars were fireflies..!

I took a moment to feel the stars, fireflies, darkness, Light and Myself...!

I can't differentiate the sky, Land, Dark and Light..!

It was as if these are one...as if I'm one among them..!

I felt i am one in the Oneness..! We become a single entity..!

It was as if we all become One...!!!!!!

Will you be a reality someday...??!!

Is it because of my emotional vacuum..?

Is it because of my longing to be loved...?

Longing to be hugged and being understood..??

Or is it just an alternative reality that

I'm cooking inside my mind..??

Or is it an escape to run away

from my suffocative reality..??

Is it a fantasy I'm building to defeat the

untrimmed jungle inside my mind...???

Is it a way I'm making to come out

from the dense forest of thoughts...??

Is it a mirage that lost people see in the desert...??

As I'm also lost in the trap of life..!

What is this i don't know..!

But having you in my thoughts brings a smile..!

Your thoughts bring me the feel of being loved...being understood...!!!

Is it Love..?? Am i in love with you..?? Are we soul mates..???

Is it just because it is meant to be..??!!

Will you be a reality someday...?

Or will you be vanished from my mind

just like a passing thought...?

Will you be a reality someday..?

Or will you be just a mirage in a desert..??

Will you be a reality someday...???

Or will be remain just a confusion of a struggling mind..????

Who is more beautiful..??

They are everywhere...all beautiful and refreshing..!

The young are beautiful and energetic..!

And the old are graceful and wise..!

The young are looking forward with their shining skins and naiveness..!

And the old are looking backward with their wisdom and experience..!

My nest in Tezu is surrounded by these beauties.....!

One day, I heard them discussing "who is more beautiful...?"

The young beauties said; "I've shining leaves...I bear fruits...

I'm decorated with flowers...birds come to me..

I'm lively and refreshing..! So, I'm more beautiful..."!!!!

"I've no shining leaves anymore...my branches are also weak...

And I'm without fruits and flowers..!

But I'm filled with wisdom, experience and patience..!

So, I'm more beautiful...""!!! Said the old beauties..!

Being unable to decide who is more beautiful they asked me..!

"You're the most beautiful creature..!

What can be more beautiful than you..!

You both are one..! The young beautiful one is the past...

And the old beautiful one is the future...

You are the most beautiful creature my friend..!!!

I replied to the trees..!!

She still loves everyone..!

She was without scars and blemishes...

she was so refreshing and young..!

She was so full of life...she wasn't wounded..!

She was resting in the lap of serenity and purity..!

Oh yes..! She herself was a manifestation of peace and kindness..!

She accepted all...she gave shelter to all..!

And she had loved all..!

I met many beautiful hearts here...many compassionate people I met here..!

After sixteen years I'm back to her...!

But my homecoming became a nightmare..!

I saw that time has been cruel to her..!

She is getting old and sick with scar and blemishes on her whole body..!

She is wounded..! her liveliness has gone...

her soul soothing peacefulness has gone..!

The mustard blooming is gone...!

Now crowdedness is shouting at quietness...!

Gone are the days when the houses and lanes looks like

as if an expert artist has drawn a beautiful pattern..!

Those clear and visible houses are gone..!

Now "Barriers" are shouting at openness..!

Houses are closed with walls as if everyone is hiding something...

as if darkness and secrecy is defeating clarity and openness..!

The walled houses are ruining the beautiful pattern..!

Oh she is wounded...she is uglified...she is hurt..!!

When i was back to her i feel as if she was embracing me with her smile..!

She was smiling but smiling a sad smile..!

I loved her so much that i was praying unceasingly to be back to her..!

Though crowded and noisy...though wounded

her heart is so calm and spacious..!

She still embraces everyone and everything..!

She still loves everyone...Yes! Tezu still loves everyone..!

Her kindness...her gracefulness...

her purity will defeat the 'crowdedness' and 'scars'...

Someday...!!!!!

My story teller is gone..!

I'm your legacy so I'll be your image now..!

I'm what you have taught me so I'll be your projection..!

I'll be the projection of your upbringing..!

Grandmother! I'll be your continuation..!

I'll tell the world the stories you've told me..!

I'll bring smile to faces as you've brought to ours..!

I'll continue the laughter we shared

while listening the stories of yours..!

My grand mother...my story teller! Now you're gone..!

But never be sad because I'll be you in "Here"...!

Be a story teller "There"...!

And continue to share love and laughter there..!

Here, I'll be your continuation...I'll be the story teller..!

Yes, in "Here" I'll be you now...!

Spreading Love and laughter through my stories and Poetry..!

And I'll resurrect your stories and songs..!!!!!

The Thirty eight springs...!

The thirty eight springs has gone unnoticed..!

The blooming it brings has gone unappreciated..!

The wounds were young and painful..!

The wounds were stinging and burning..!

As if it was the summer bringing me only flooding..!

The summer blocked my way to the springs and the blooming..!

The thirty eight summers has consumed my thirty eight springs..!!!!!

An empty grave...somewhere..!

And someday I'll reach my last days....!

I heard funerals are also expensive these days..!

I'll need a land to be buried one day..!

But I don't have land...so it will be a funeral of a

Landless person..!

I will be worried about the land for my grave..!

Then, I will tell my soul there is an 'empty grave' somewhere..!

Let the Lovers live..!

Let the lovers live...let the lovers love..!

They are harmless because they are lovers..!

They are lost..! Lost in love..! They are harmless..!

Let the lovers love the Love in any form..!

Don't kill them for honour...!

Don't kill them for pride..!

They are death already..!

Lovers are killed by love already..!

But now I'm in Love..!

I thought Love is easy....And good..!

I thought Love is interesting...And fine...!

And will bring smile..!

So, I decided to be a lover...!

But now I'm in Love...And I'm a lover now..!

I lost my own heart...And senses..!

As if my heart got wings...And it flies away..!

Now, I know love is so demanding...And consuming...!!!!

Mr. Blue Sky and the White Dove..!!

He is so vast...he is so big...!

He has everything...everyone is under him..!

I'm so tiny...he may not want me..! He may not love me..!

Think the white Dove..!

The white Dove is in Love with Mr. Blue Sky..!

She is intoxicated by his handsome blueness..!

But there are clouds everywhere...So, she thinks

"I'll lose amidst these clouds and will never reach him..."!!

"I wish she could sit on the clouds and reach me..."!

Thinks the Mr. Blue Sky..!

She is so beautiful...she is so true, pure and graceful..!

Every beauty is in her..! Thinks Mr. Blue Sky..!

Mr. Blue Sky is also in love with the white Dove..!

He needs her...he longs for her presence in his life..!

I'm vast..I'm big but I'm so empty..! Thinks Mr. Blue Sky..!

Mr. Blue Sky is big and is everywhere...

White dove is small and is in obscurity..!

Separation has separated Mr. Blue Sky and the White Dove..!

But Love made them inseparable...!!!!!!!

I am a Mordecai...!

Haman is everywhere...Haman is growing fast..!

Haman is still chasing me...

Like a heavy haunting shadow Haman is chasing me...

I'll awake the Mordecai in me..!

Haman has to be stopped....stopped and ended..!!

I'm a Mordecai..! I'll raise the Mordecai in me..!!!

Haman is chasing me from generations...chasing me unceasingly...

Chasing me to push my soul in the bottomless dark pit..!!

His curse...his grudge has to be stopped...stopped and ended..!

His grip is growing fast..!

But I'm a Mordecai i will make Haman a past...

A past...not to be seen again....!!

I'm a curse-breaker because I'm a Mordecai..!

Haman will be no more...!!..Erase and annihilated perfectly..!!

I'm a Mordecai...!

And I will be the Mordecai defeating and destroying the Hamans...

The Hamans of my life..!

Yes.., i will break the 'generational curse'...

I'm a Mordecai...!

And I am here to make the Hamans a past...!!!!!